W9-DFP-005

YOUR CAREER IN THE
COAST GUARD

TAMRA B. ORR

ROSEN
PUBLISHING®
New York

Published in 2012 by The Rosen Publishing Group, Inc.
29 East 21st Street, New York, NY 10010

Copyright © 2012 by The Rosen Publishing Group, Inc.

First Edition

Library of Congress Cataloging-in-Publication Data

Orr, Tamra.
Your career in the Coast Guard / Tamra B. Orr.—1st ed.
   p. cm.—(The call of duty: careers in the armed forces)
Includes bibliographical references and index.
ISBN 978-1-4488-5514-8 (library binding)
1. United States. Coast Guard—Juvenile literature. 2.
United States. Coast Guard—Vocational guidance—Juvenile
literature. I. Title.
VG53.O775 2012
363.28'602373—dc22
                                                    2011012105

Manufactured in the United States of America

CPSIA Compliance Information: Batch #W12YA: For further information, contact Rosen Publishing, New York, New York, at 1-800-237-9932.

CONTENTS

INTRODUCTION

I n early 2011, almost a dozen fishermen near Catawba Island in Ohio were the beneficiaries of the good timing and expert seamanship of the local coast guard. All of them were lost on the ice of Lake Erie, and it took an airboat crew from the Marblehead Coast Guard Station to track them down and return them to safety. "No ice is safe ice," Lieutenant David Smith from the USCG's 9th District in Cleveland told a reporter from the *Cleveland Plain Dealer*. The group of fishermen had been caught in an unexpectedly heavy snowstorm and called 911 on their cell phones when they got lost in the blanket of white. "The snow was so heavy, they could not see their way back to the shore," Petty Officer James Hassinger explained to the *Plain Dealer*. Four fishermen were located with the coast guard's airboat. On the way back to port, the group ran into three more men who had gotten lost. Before they could reach shore, a call came in stating four more men were missing. Once found, all eleven were escorted back to safety. "We see this fairly often during the ice season, unfortunately," said Smith.

In February 2011, a coast guard cutter saved four boaters off the coast of Cape Hatteras whose vessel

A U.S. Coast Guard search and rescue team performs a search and rescue demonstration during the sixtieth annual Seattle Seafair in Seattle, Washington.

had taken on water and capsized. Later that same month, the coast guard organized and instituted a weekly beach cleanup effort in the Bahamas. This ongoing effort followed the marooning of a vessel offshore that produced a large quantity of garbage and trash—including clothes and mattresses—that washed up on local beaches. Though a reaction to a specific emergency, the coast guard's actions were all part of its institutional commitment to environmental protection and responsibility. This commitment was proved most dramatically during the coast guard's heroic efforts in the 2010 cleanup of the massive oil spill in the Gulf of Mexico following the explosion of the offshore oil well Deepwater Horizon.

These are just a few examples of the U.S. Coast Guard at work, engaging in search and rescue operations, protecting the nation's coastlines and waterways, and safeguarding the ecological health and boating safety of U.S. waters. Time and again, the U.S. Coast Guard has lived up to its motto of *Semper Paratus*, or "Always Ready." Do you want to be part of this exciting, adventurous, and high-tech military branch that serves and protects both the nation and its waterways from threats both military and environmental? Let's find out.

CHAPTER 1

SAFETY, SECURITY, AND STEWARDSHIP

Latitude
Longitude

44° 49' 6"
20° 28'

Have you been thinking about joining the military? It is a question that many young people consider, and with good reason. It is not a small-scale, casual life decision, like whether or not to take a part-time job at the local car wash or whether to spend your spring break with the family in Florida or hang out with friends at home. Joining the military is a major decision because it requires a great deal of time and commitment. One way to make the decision easier is by taking the time to ask a lot of questions and do as much research as you can. Making up your mind about your future is far easier when you have all the facts at your disposal.

Take a moment to think about the five different branches of the armed forces. Chances are the navy, army, air force, and marines all came to mind before the coast guard did. That isn't too surprising. The coast guard is much smaller than the other branches,

Petty Officer 1st Class Noreen Carroll, a marine science technician, talks to students from Tidewater Community College in Portsmouth, Virginia, about career and education opportunities in the coast guard.

averaging just over 42,000 enlisted personnel and officers, compared to the army's 539,675 or the navy's 326,684. Many people have heard of the coast guard, but when asked what the organization actually does, they commonly draw a blank.

Learning about the history of the coast guard can help you understand why this military branch exists and what an essential role it plays in the nation's security and protection.

THE COAST GUARD THROUGHOUT HISTORY

The coast guard is actually a combination of several different organizations that have merged over the last 250 years. It has been under the control of the U.S. Department of the Treasury, the Justice Department, and even the Department of Transportation.

The coast guard's origins as a lighthouse service are shown by this seal. In the past, members of the service were primarily charged with operating and maintaining the nation's lighthouses and other navigation aids.

The coast guard got its start in 1789 as the U.S. Lighthouse Service, but by the following year, it had become the Revenue Marine. It was first created by Alexander Hamilton to enforce laws regarding what cargo could and could not be carried into and out of American waters. Vessels were sent out to prevent smuggling and enforce trade laws. By 1838, the Justice Department had stepped in and changed the focus of the organization to one of keeping the passengers on steam-powered vessels safe. The group's new name was the Steamboat Inspection Service. It wasn't until 1915, when President Woodrow Wilson signed into law the Coast Guard Act, that the service's twin duties of life-saving and revenue policy enforcement (enforcing trade and tariff laws) were combined.

Just two years later, American involvement in World War I began, and the coast guard found itself under the jurisdiction of the U.S. Navy. Over the next few decades, the coast guard absorbed the Lighthouse Service and the Bureau of Marine Inspection and Navigation. As a result, its duties expanded to include assisting and maintaining the nation's aids to maritime navigation, including operating the country's lighthouses and overseeing the safety and licensing of America's merchant marine.

In 2003, the coast guard became an official part of the Department of Homeland Security (DHS). During times of peace, the coast guard is under the jurisdiction of the DHS. During times of war, however, it serves under the Department of the Navy. At all times, the U.S. Coast Guard serves as the nation's frontline agency for enforcing laws at sea, protecting the marine environment and the nation's vast coastline and ports, and saving lives.

A DIFFERENT KIND OF BRANCH

How does the coast guard differ from the other branches of the military? Clearly, it is much smaller, and because of that, officials believe it has a more "family-friendly" atmosphere. Chief Aviation

Maintenance Technician Russell Kirkham, a recruiter for the states of Oregon and Washington, confirmed this in an interview with the author. "In the coast guard, you aren't just a single person among tens of thousands. You are names to us, not numbers. We are like the Little Engine That Could. We try harder."

The coast guard does just what its name implies: it guards the nation's shorelines. Its primary goals are to protect the public, environment, and security of the country's coasts, ports, and waterways. It does this by focusing on eleven core missions that fall under the headings of maritime safety, security, and stewardship. These missions include:

- Search and rescue
- Marine safety
- Ports, waterways, and coastal security
- Drug interdiction (disrupting of illegal drug trafficking activity and seizure of drugs)
- Migrant interdiction (detaining of illegal migration of peoples and illegal human trafficking)
- Defense readiness
- Ice operations
- Aids to navigation
- Marine environmental protection
- Living marine resources
- Other law enforcement

The coast guard's focus on maritime security, safety, and stewardship is evident in every one of the actions performed by its servicemen and women, every day of the year.

Its responsibility for maritime security means that the coast guard is literally "the law of the sea" and has been since its creation in 1790. The coast guard helps keep the nation safe by stopping both undocumented immigrants and illegal drugs from entering the United States via its waterways. Between the coast guard's aircraft and ships, the service intercepts thousands of tons of cocaine and marijuana and thousands of illegal immigrants every year. The coast guard patrols harbors looking for any possible problems, such as terrorist activity. It also deploys its cutters and other boats and aircraft to help with any Department of Defense operations.

Search and rescue missions fall under the coast guard's mandate to ensure maritime safety. In 2008, it engaged in more than twenty-four thousand search and rescue operations, saving over four thousand lives in the process. The coast guard also investigates accidents at sea; inspects merchant vessels, offshore drilling units, and marine facilities; and teaches and implements a variety of water and boat safety programs.

The coast guard's maritime stewardship responsibilities include not only protecting people at sea but also the natural resources of the waterways

A Visit, Board, Search, and Seizure (VBSS) Team from U.S. Coast Guard Law Enforcement prepares to board a vessel suspected of smuggling drugs during an antidrug operation conducted south of Jamaica.

themselves. To help safeguard those waters, the coast guard performs thousands of safety inspections and investigations of any maritime accidents that result in pollution. The coast guard protects U.S. fishing grounds by making sure that foreign fishermen are not illegally harvesting America's fish stocks. One day coast guard members may be freeing an entangled whale, while the next day they are cleaning up the buoys, lighthouses, and beacons that are the ocean's "traffic signals." They also help contain and clean up

The Canadian Coast Guard Ship *Louis S. St-Laurent* makes an approach to the U.S. Coast Guard cutter *Healy* in the Arctic Ocean. The two ships were taking part in a multiyear, multiagency Arctic survey that would help define the Arctic continental shelf.

oil spills and work to prevent the illegal dumping of plastics and other garbage into the nation's waters.

In addition, the coast guard operates polar ice-breakers—special ships that cut through ice in the Arctic and Antarctic regions, helping to keep shipping lanes open. These polar operations ensure that ships can move through the area safely year-round. They also monitor sea traffic in the Arctic and defend the country's interests in those waters.

REASONS TO BECOME A GUARDIAN

Some people want to enlist in the coast guard because of the steady income the military can provide. In an often uncertain economy, a regular paycheck is something to value, and coast guard service members are paid twice a month without fear of being laid off. Others choose to join because of the benefits, including the medical and dental care offered. Still others are intrigued by the education and training a career in the coast guard can provide. An education is expensive, and finding a way to help serve and protect the country while being paid to learn and receive professional training is a win-win combination for many people.

Perhaps adventure is more of what you had in mind. You want to travel and see the world. Both are strong reasons for becoming part of the coast guard.

This service gives enlistees—men and women alike—the chance to learn, develop career skills, and have adventures all at the same time.

Of course, some people have a very simple reason for wanting to join the coast guard: they simply want to help serve and protect their country. Patriotism is another great reason for enlisting. Chances are your personal reasons are some of these combined.

Are you curious about who makes up the coast guard? Here is the most recent breakdown to help you get a good picture:

FACT	TOTAL
Number of enlisted	34,134
Number of officers	8,255
Percentage of men	86.9
Percentage of women	13.1
Percentage of African Americans	5.6
Percentage of Caucasians	77.4
Percentage of Asian	0.8
Percentage of Hispanic/Latino	11.0

"CREED OF THE UNITED STATES COAST GUARDSMAN": COAST GUARD VALUES

Like the other branches of the military, the coast guard has its own personal creed that sums up what it is all

10 QUESTIONS TO ASK A
COAST GUARD RECRUITER

1. Do I need parental permission to join the coast guard?
2. How does the coast guard differ from other branches of the military?
3. How long am I committed to serve in the coast guard?
4. What skills do I need to have to be admitted?
5. What tests are required to be part of the coast guard?
6. What is boot camp like, and how long does it last?
7. Why does the coast guard often work with the marines and the navy?
8. Where will I most likely be stationed, and am I likely to see combat?
9. How much time is spent out on the water?
10. What kinds of military and civilian careers are open to me through coast guard service?

about. As you read it over, think about what taking such a pledge might mean in your life. How would these promises guide your behavior and attitudes?

I am proud to be a United States Coast Guardsman.

I revere that long line of expert seamen who by their devotion to duty and a sacrifice of self have made it possible for me to be a member of a service honored and respected, in peace and in war, throughout the world.

I never, by word or deed, will bring reproach upon the fair name of my service, nor permit others to do so unchallenged.

I will cheerfully and willingly obey all lawful orders.

I will always be on time to relieve, and shall endeavor to do more, rather than less, than my share.

I will always be at my station, alert and attending to my duties.

I shall, so far as I am able, bring to my seniors solutions, not problems.

I shall live joyously, but always with due regard to the rights and privileges of others.

I shall endeavor to be a model citizen in the community in which I live.

I shall sell life dearly to an enemy of my country, but give it freely to rescue those in peril.

With God's help, I shall endeavor to be one of his Noblest Works.

This oath echoes what the coast guard says
are its core values: honor, respect, and devotion to
duty. As stated in *The Coast Guard Officer Career
Development Guidebook*:

VALUE	DEFINITION
Honor	Integrity is our standard. We demonstrate uncompromising ethical conduct and moral behavior in all our personal actions. We are loyal and accountable to the public trust.
Respect	We value our diverse work force. We treat each other with fairness, dignity, and compassion. We encourage individual opportunity and growth. We encourage creativity through empowerment. We work as a team.
Devotion to Duty	We are professionals, military and civilian, who seek responsibility, accept accountability, and are committed to the successful achievement of our organizational goals. We exist to serve. We serve with pride.

ENLISTED OR OFFICER?

Another question to ponder as you consider joining the coast guard is whether you want to enter as
an enlisted man or woman or as an officer. Enlisted

guardians do not require a college degree to perform their jobs within the coast guard. Instead, they are taught on the job in a wide variety of skills, jobs, and career paths, from aviation to law enforcement. This on-the-job training is enhanced with tests and evaluations administered by the experts who teach and train guard members. All of the skills you learn transfer easily to the civilian world after your term of service as a guardian is over.

Officers, on the other hand, either attend and graduate from the Coast Guard Academy or complete Officer Candidate School. The Coast Guard Academy is located in New London, Connecticut. About three hundred high school graduates are enrolled there each year. After four years, they graduate with a bachelor of science degree and earn the rank of ensign. Officer Candidate School is also located in New London. It is highly selective, and getting in is often quite competitive. The course takes seventeen weeks to complete. Studies include nautical science, law enforcement, seamanship, and leadership classes. Applicants to the Officer Candidate School must be at least twenty-one years old, be a senior in college or already have earned a college degree, and have earned a qualifying score on the SAT or ACT and the ASVAB aptitude tests.

Enlisting in the coast guard means signing a contract that commits you to eight years of service. The first four of these years are active duty, while

Newly commissioned officers celebrate their graduation from the U.S. Coast Guard Academy in New London, Connecticut.

the remaining four are on a reserve basis. This is a major commitment and one that takes a great deal of thought. What are the risks? Who does the coast guard take—and who doesn't it accept, and why? Once in, what are the possible career pathways for young men and women? These are excellent questions and ones that require answers before you sign your name on any dotted line. Time to find out!

CHAPTER 2

GETTING STARTED IN THE COAST GUARD

You've made the decision. The coast guard is the military branch that is calling to you the loudest. You know you want to be a part of it—but are you eligible? What does it take to be a part of this elite group?

"We are very selective in who joins us," Chief Aviation Maintenance Technician Kirkham told the author in an interview. "Out of 150 or 200 applicants, we typically take one or two." According to the coast guard's Web site, the organization has very high standards. In 2009, only 5,500 people were accepted into the service. Unlike other military branches, the coast guard demands that applicants not only meet set requirements but also be evaluated as a "whole person," including an assessment of the applicant's passion for joining and potential for developing leadership qualities.

MEETING THE REQUIREMENTS

The basic criteria for a coast guard applicant are as follows:

- You must be a U.S. citizen or a resident alien.
- You must be between the ages of seventeen and thirty-four (seventeen-year-olds will need parental permission).
- Reservists must be between the ages of seventeen and thirty-nine.
- You must have a high school diploma. GEDs are accepted only in special circumstances.
- You must not have more than two dependents.

If you meet all of these requirements, you are one step closer to successfully enlisting in the coast guard. However, this is only the first of many steps.

Next, you have to fill out an application and send it to the local recruiting office. Once it is reviewed, you will be contacted for an interview. Some of the questions found on the initial application include:

- Can you swim? If not, can you be taught to swim? Swimming ability is not required; the ability to learn is.

Basic training in the coast guard includes physical fitness tests that incorporate running, swimming, and lots of sit-ups, push-ups, and pull-ups.

- Are you now, or have you ever been, a conscientious objector?
- Have you ever received the Boy Scouts' Eagle Scout Award or the Girl Scouts' Gold Award?
- Do you have any tattoos? Explain (by filling out the Tattoo Screening Form, which includes tattoos, brands, body piercing, and intentional scarring or self-mutilations).

The next step is making sure that you can pass the physical fitness assessment. This examines your capacity for aerobic activity, your muscular strength, and your overall endurance. If you can't do all of this yet, don't worry. Boot camp will get you fully up to speed physically. The following chart shows what the coast guard uses as its standards:

EVENT	MALE	FEMALE
Number of push-ups in 60 seconds	29	15
Number of sit-ups in 60 seconds	38	32
Run 1.5 miles (2.4 kilometers)	12 minutes, 51 seconds	15 minutes, 26 seconds
Sit and reach (Sit with feet and legs together and reach toward feet. Measurement is taken from your knees to your feet.)	16.5 inches (42 centimeters) past your knees	19.29 inches (49 cm) past your knees
Complete swim circuit test	Tread water for 5 minutes	
	Jump off 5-foot (1.5 meters) platform into pool and swim 109 yards (100 m)	

Next, a police background and credit check will be done. Second- and third-degree misdemeanors and any felony convictions disqualify you. Your financial history is also an important factor. These background checks are followed by the "whole person" evaluation, which assesses your attitude, professionalism, honesty, respect, language proficiency, weight, physical abilities, and work ethic. The coast guard also has height and weight requirements for both men and women based on overall frame size.

TAKING THE ASVAB

All applicants to the coast guard must pass a test called the Armed Services Vocational Aptitude Battery (ASVAB). This test is required for all of the military branches. It is not designed to measure your intelligence but your aptitude or ability to perform different kinds of jobs. It provides invaluable information to help you and your counselor determine which career path within the coast guard is best for you. There are a total of two hundred questions on the test, covering four general academic fields: science, arithmetic reasoning, word knowledge, and paragraph comprehension. The test also covers five career subjects: auto and shop information, mathematics knowledge, electronics information, mechanical comprehension, and assembling objects. It takes about three hours to complete all of the tests.

The minimum score for coast guard admittance is 45, the highest required score of all of the service branches. There are numerous sites online that provide sample test questions to help you prepare and practice for this test. In the meantime, here are some

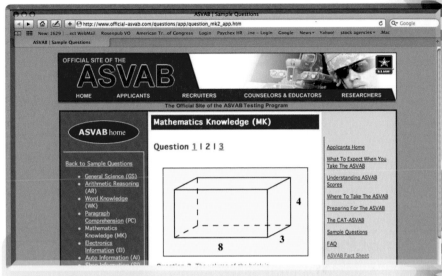

A sample question from the ASVAB exam appears above (http://www.official-asvab.com). The ASVAB measures developed abilities and helps predict future academic and occupational success in the military. It is administered annually to more than one million military applicants, high school, and postsecondary students.

sample questions from each section of the test (these questions are taken from the practice site http://www.official-asvab.com/questions/app/question_mk2_app.htm). The correct answer has an asterisk next to it.

General Science

Air is less dense than water because:

1. It is lighter
2. Its molecules are farther apart *
3. Its molecules are closer together
4. It moves more quickly and easily

Arithmetic Reasoning

If the tire of a car rotates at a constant speed of 552 times in one minute, how many times will the tire rotate in half an hour?

1. 276
2. 5,520
3. 8,280
4. 16,560 *

Word Knowledge

Antagonize most nearly means

1. Embarrass
2. Struggle
3. Provoke *
4. Worship

Paragraph Comprehension

"The eastern part of Texas will ambush the senses of all who enter it with preconceptions of sand and cacti around every bend. It has a look and atmosphere that does not fit the boots-and-saddle image of the state."

The author implies that the look and atmosphere of east Texas do NOT resemble that of the

1. Marshlands
2. Mountains

3. Seashore

4. Desert ✳

Mathematics Knowledge

The volume of the brick is

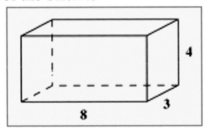

1. 15
2. 36
3. 44
4. 96 ✳

Electronics Information

Because solid state diodes have no filament, they

1. Don't work
2. Are less efficient than tubes
3. Require less operating power ✳
4. Require more operating power

Auto Information

Shock absorbers on a car connect the axle to the

1. Wheel
2. Chassis ✳
3. Drive shaft
4. Exhaust pipe

Shop Information

Sanding blocks are used to

1. Prevent high spots and ridges on sanded surfaces *
2. Prevent dirt from collecting on the sandpaper
3. Stretch the length of the sandpaper
4. Prolong the use of the sandpaper

Mechanical Comprehension

Extending the reach of this crane will shift its

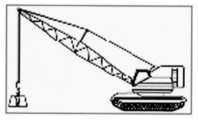

1. Total weight
2. Allowable speed
3. Center of gravity *
4. Center of buoyancy

Assembling Objects

Which figure best shows how the objects in the left box will appear if they are fit together?

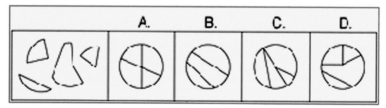

1. A
2. B.
3. C
4. D ⁕

BOOT CAMP SURVIVAL

Hollywood has spent years making movies that show military boot camp as extraordinarily difficult and exhausting, and for the most part, that depiction is pretty accurate. Basic training is challenging for both mind and body. Recruits spend almost eight weeks at Cape May, in New Jersey, learning about the coast guard and getting into shape.

The first few days of boot camp are spent settling in at Sexton Hall, where new recruits stay. When the bus pulls into the base, recruits are likely to hear something along these lines, shouted at high volume by a company commander, "Welcome to Cape May. The first thing you're gonna do is shut up, sit up, and take your hats off . . . You're gonna do what I say, when I say it, and how I say to do it . . . You've got ten seconds to get off this bus, and you've just wasted three."

Next, recruits are issued their uniforms, figure out where everything is on the base, fill out lots of paperwork, and, of course, get haircuts. They provide urine samples for drug and alcohol tests, get medical and dental screenings, and a number of vaccination shots. Their living area is called a squad bay, and they are expected to keep it immaculate at all times.

Recruits are allowed to bring only certain things to boot camp with them, such as civilian clothing, toiletries, medications, and writing utensils. They are allowed to stow personal items like cameras, address books, watches, wallets, and keys in a bag in storage. They may not bring tobacco products, food, beverages, newspapers or magazines, or any weapons. They will be provided with most of what they need, including items like hangers, shampoo, soap, deodorant, tooth-paste, pens, and paper. Their personal possessions are inspected to make sure that recruits have brought only approved items. Any items not on the list of approved personal effects will be seized. A recruit's day begins at 5:30 AM, and lights go out at 10:00 PM sharp.

New recruits are soon introduced to their company commander. This person will fill many roles, from leader and coach to guide and mentor. It is his or her job to keep recruits motivated and teach them to obey orders. It won't always be an easy relationship, but recruits certainly learn and benefit from it. If they make a mistake in boot camp, the response is almost certainly going to be getting yelled at, at maximum volume. That is part of the training process, and the treatment is designed to help recruits develop self-discipline.

Coast Guard Chief Petty Officer George Bou, a company commander, disciplines a new recruit at the Coast Guard Training Center in Cape May, New Jersey. Recruits are often yelled at and pushed extremely hard until they conform to military standards.

Remember those physical fitness standards discussed before? By the time recruits finish their eight weeks in basic training, they will be able to meet all of them. Boot camp gets you into shape quickly!

Of course, academic training is part of boot camp also. Recruits take classes such as Uniform Code of Military Justice; Military Civil Rights; Stress Management; Coast Guard Chain of Command,

Rates, and Ranks; Addressing Military Personnel; Military Pay and Allowances; and Coast Guard History, Mission, and Traditions. The fourth week of boot camp features classes in Classified Materials, Vessels and Aircraft, and Performance Evaluations. In addition, there are obstacle courses to conquer and instruction in small arms and basic pistol use. A midterm examination is administered, and a physical test is given to make sure that recruits meet all the coast guard's requirements.

The fifth week of boot camp continues with a variety of classes, including Survival Equipment, Coast Guard Terms, Ethical Conduct, Flags and Pennants, and Emergency Drills. The sixth week focuses on firefighting education, as well as career counseling. The seventh week includes a final exam. Recruits receive their assignments, and then it is time to graduate. The successful recruits march in a parade, awards are handed out, and then everyone is released to go out and celebrate.

To get an idea of what boot camp is like for the coast guard recruits, check out the USCG's Media Port Web site, which features videos of basic training and interviews with recruits. The site can be found online at http://www.uscgbootcamp.com. The Web site for the training center can be found at http://www.uscg.mil/hq/capemay. In addition, the *Guardian Handbook* that all recruits are given during training can also be found at this site.

New recruits learn how to extinguish a shipboard fire at the Coast Guard Training Center in Cape May, New Jersey. Recruits practice the procedure before donning fire protection gear and entering a completely dark and fog-filled room. This is the final test before basic fire fighting training is completed.

FIRST ASSIGNMENTS

Once the application process is over and boot camp has been survived, what is next? Recruits are sent off to their first assignment. What jobs will they perform? They may not be sure yet. Unlike the other military branches, the coast guard does not immediately place recruits into a specific career slot.

ON THE OTHER HAND...

The experiences, rewards, and benefits of serving one's nation in the coast guard or any of the other branches of the armed forces can be enormous and extremely valuable to the recruit's personal and professional development. Yet there are also some distinct potential downsides that should be realistically weighed and considered before making a commitment to serve. Just as you thoroughly researched the potential benefits of serving and debated your reasons for joining the coast guard, make sure that you consider just as seriously some of the possible reasons not to join up. Any important life decision should include a careful and conscientious consideration of the pros and cons. Some potential cons include:

- Your life can be in danger:
  Although the coast guard is not often at the forefront of combat and armed hostilities, service still does carry risk. Troops frequently provide support for the navy, and coast guard ships are commonly involved in skirmishes with pirates, smugglers, and other potentially violent people. Plus, deadly storms and fatal accidents are always a possibility aboard a ship and on the high seas.
- You can be seriously injured:
  See above.
- You will be separated for a period of weeks to years from your family and friends:

It can be very hard to be hundreds or even thousands of miles away from the people you love and care about the most. For some recruits, homesickness is very difficult to overcome. Even if your spouse and children are stationed near you, if you are on a ship for months at a time, the distance can be a real strain.

- You are dedicating eight years of your life to the coast guard:
Eight years is a long time and a very big commitment. Even though only four years of the commitment are active, these are prime years of your life and ones that you may want to spend in college or working in the civilian world instead.

- You cannot quit even if you don't like it or it doesn't meet your expectations:
Once you are in the military, getting out of it is extremely difficult. Unlike a job that you can quit if you find you don't like the people or the responsibilities, the military is a contracted commitment that usually has to be kept.

- You will have to take and follow orders at all times:
Taking orders and doing whatever you are told whenever you are told is easier for some people than others. Are you sure this is something you can do without anger or resentment? Are you able to be a team player regardless of how difficult or inexplicable or seemingly pointless the chore or mission is or how much you disagree with it? If so, then the coast guard or any other military branch might work out well for you. If not, enlistment might turn into a tremendous obstacle.

Instead, they will spend the next six months experiencing all kinds of jobs. This exposure to a wide range of jobs will help new recruits identify which ones they enjoy and show aptitude for—both keys to achieving success within the coast guard and later in life.

It should also be noted that members of the coast guard serve wherever their skills are most needed. This can include service on ships or land stations throughout the United States, including Alaska and Hawaii, the Caribbean, Puerto Rico, Guam, and even Europe, Asia, and the Middle East. Most guard members serve within the United States, however. If you choose to become a reservist, you'll usually serve close to home; however, you may get deployed when necessary. In general, reservists live within 100 miles (160 km) of their coast guard reserve unit. For information on salaries and benefits associated with each coast guard job discussed in this book, and to get a list of the locations of all coast guard units and where they serve, go to the U.S. Coast Guard's official Web site, http://www.uscg.mil. Here you will also find extremely detailed listings of required qualifications, personal characteristics, training and education, duties, and locations associated with each job offered within the coast guard. Information regarding the professional paths open to you in the civilian world upon leaving the service is also available there.

CHAPTER 3

CAREERS IN THE DECK AND ORDNANCE GROUP

The operation of all the many coast guard vessels and their weaponry is a massive undertaking that requires a huge number of people highly skilled in doing different jobs. These jobs all fall under the category of the deck and ordnance group, and enlisted guardians often choose this career path. The jobs within this field from which they can choose include boatswain's mate, gunner's mate, maritime enforcement specialist, operations specialist, and intelligence specialist.

BOATSWAIN'S MATE (BM)

If you've ever met a "jack of all trades," or someone who seems to know how to do a little of bit of absolutely everything, then you have an idea of what a boatswain's (pronounced bo-sun's) mate does. The boatswain's mate is often considered to be one of the most flexible and multiskilled members on the entire

A boatswain's mate lowers a small boat using the starboard boat davit onboard the coast guard cutter *Bertholf*, stationed in the Gulf of Mexico.

coast guard team. If you enjoy a job that keeps you busy with a wide variety of duties, this enlisted position might be a good fit for you.

The boatswain's mate works on all kinds of ships and boats, from a coast guard cutter to a harbor tug, a patrol boat to an icebreaker. Occasionally, you will even double as a federal law enforcement officer. Some of your job responsibilities as a BM will include:

• Operating hoists, cranes, and winches for activities like loading cargo or putting gangplanks into position
• Standing watch for security
• Navigating at sea
• Supervising personnel on a ship's deck force

- General knowledge of ropes and cables, including different uses, stresses, strains, and proper stowing

What skills does this type of job require? Physical strength is important, as well as above-average manual dexterity. The training for this position is twelve weeks long. Once completed, boatswain's mates can then go on to advanced training in a variety of related fields such as coxswain, heavy weather coxswain, or buoy deck supervisor.

GUNNER'S MATE (GM)

If you are intrigued by weaponry and explosives, you might consider becoming a gunner's mate. This enlisted job is one of the coast guard's oldest, dating all the way back to 1797. A gunner's mate, as the name implies, is someone who works with all kinds of weaponry. You will be the person who trains everyone in how to handle pistols, rifles, and machine guns, plus ammunition and pyrotechnics. In addition, you will be trained in skills such as:

- Electronics
- Mechanical systems
- Hydraulics
- Maintenance on ordnance/gunnery equipment

A gunner's mate replaces the barrel on an M-240 machine gun aboard the coast guard cutter *Legare*. The cutter also features M-60 machine guns and a 76mm deck gun.

Gunner's mates are trained in Yorktown, Virginia, for ten weeks, followed by another fourteen weeks of specific training on a particular type of weaponry system. Clearly, an interest and ability in mechanics and mathematics, plus a familiarity with different kinds of small arms, are helpful for this position.

MARITIME ENFORCEMENT SPECIALIST (ME)

If you can imagine what it would be like to be a police officer out on the water, then you will have some idea of what a maritime enforcement specialist does. These enlisted guardians are given the duties of:

- Traditional maritime law enforcement
- Antiterrorism force protection
- Port security and safety
- Physical security
- Unit-level training in all of the above

The coast guard patrols a lagoon in advance of the launch of the space shuttle *Discovery* at the Kennedy Space Center in Florida.

Someone with a background in law enforcement or security will do best in this field, and experience with firearms is a plus. A spotless criminal record is also a requirement.

OPERATIONS SPECIALIST (OS)

Are you a detail-oriented person with a talent for organization? Would you be able to make important decisions that affect the lives of many others without getting too stressed or rattled in the process? If so, this might be the right career path for you. An operations specialist is considered a command and control expert. Operations specialists perform a central role in the execution of nearly all coast guard operations. Operations specialists coordinate responses to a wide variety of coast guard missions, including search and rescue, maritime law enforcement, marine environmental protection, homeland security, and national defense. They also operate state-of-the-art communication systems, tactical tracking and identification systems, shipboard navigation systems, and advanced operational planning applications.

Operations specialists are stationed throughout the coast guard, serving primarily at command centers and aboard larger cutters around the United States, including Alaska, Hawaii, Puerto Rico, and Guam. An OS can expect to participate in all aspects of operational planning and execution, working with decision makers and operators to accomplish coast guard missions twenty-four hours a day. A job in this field means extensive training in communication systems and the software used for missions and operations. It is often a high-stress job, so keeping calm in the face of pressure is a must.

INTELLIGENCE SPECIALIST (IS)

Do you enjoy gathering and analyzing information, decoding meaning from reams of data, and trying to anticipate an opponent's motives or next moves? If so, you might consider pursuing a career as a coast

THE ART OF VERTICAL INSERTION TRAINING

One of the coast guard's main jobs is to inspect other ships. How guardsmen and women do it, however, can sometimes be quite daunting. They slide down a rope 30 feet (9 m) from a helicopter to the ship's deck below. This is known as a vertical insertion. It is a tricky maneuver requiring specific skill and training. "It's not as simple as sliding down a rope," lead instructor Steve McDonald explained to Luke Pinnero of the Coast Guard News Service.

Vertical insertion training begins by testing the guardians' upper-body strength through pull-ups and chin-ups—while wearing full gear. Then they are taken to the top of a 50-foot (15 m) tower from which a green rope dangles to the ground below. Guardians get used to going down the tower, but they all know it is not the same thing as doing it from a helicopter. "You're deploying from a helicopter with a lot of moving parts, onto a ship with a lot of moving parts," Lieutenant Paul Casey, told Pinnero, an instructor. In addition to learning how to slide down the rope and land safely, students go through a grueling water survival course that involves a trainer chair that turns them upside down.

By the end of the training, the guardians can rush onto the deck of a ship in a matter of seconds. "Our teams are very well-qualified, once our feet hit the deck, to control pretty much any situation that we're put into," adds McDonald.

guard intelligence specialist. The intelligence specialist performs a wide range of duties associated with
the collection, analysis, processing, and dissemination
of intelligence in support of coast guard operational
missions. Although you will most likely be stationed
at the Intelligence Coordination Center, you may also
be placed in air units or on a ship at sea. The duties of
the IS are many, including:

- Identifying and producing intelligence from
  basic data
- Assembling and analyzing multisource oper-
  ational intelligence
- Collecting and analyzing communication
  signals through computer technology
- Providing input to and receiving informa-
  tion from many different computer systems
- Preparing and presenting intelligence brief-
  ings to those in charge
- Compiling planning materials for opera-
  tional missions
- Holding mission debriefings
- Analyzing results
- Preparing reports, graphics, overlays, pho-
  tos, and maps
- Plotting sources on maps and charts
- Maintaining intelligence databases, librar-
  ies, and files

Two coast guard petty officers monitor the Automatic Identification System (AIS) at Maritime Intelligence Fusion Center Atlantic in Virginia Beach, Virginia. The AIS is a system required for all commercial vessels weighing three hundred or more gross tons, which broadcasts their identification, position, course, speed, and other information.

To learn how to do all of this, enlisted guardians attend thirteen weeks of training in Yorktown, Virginia. Many intelligence specialists choose to go beyond this basic training to more advanced studies.

One of the most recognized hallmarks of the coast guard is its many types of ships and aircraft and the weaponry associated with them. By being part of the Deck and Ordnance division, you will have a chance to know how these machines and weapons work inside and out. You may also have the opportunity to handle some of the top-secret information that keeps the coast guard's fleet safe on the water.

CHAPTER 4

CAREERS IN THE HULL AND ENGINEERING GROUP

Do you like to figure out how machines and equipment run? Are you interested in taking a blueprint and turning it into reality? Are you a hands-on person? Opting for a job within the coast guard's hull and engineering group may be a great choice for you. Work within this group centers upon the upkeep and operation of coast guard vessels. The jobs within this group include damage controlman, electrician's mate, electrician's technician, information system technician, and machinery technician.

DAMAGE CONTROLMAN (DC)

Damage controlmen are the coast guard's repairmen and maintenance specialists. If you have already learned some basic construction skills, along with welding or plumbing, becoming a DC might be a simple process for you. You will be the person everyone will

48

look to when something breaks or is damaged on board a ship. Whether it is a leaking pipe or a small engine fire that needs to be contained and extinguished, you will be in demand. Damage controlmen are placed on cutters, buoy tenders, and river tenders, where they focus on jobs such as:

A damage controlman on board the coast guard cutter *Oak* welds repairs on a coast guard dock in Haiti.

- Maintaining watertight integrity of vessels (no leaks allowed!)
- Maintaining and repairing emergency equipment used for firefighting and flooding
- Plumbing repairs
- Welding repairs
- Firefighting
- Carpentry
- Chemical, biological, and nuclear-warfare detection and decontamination

The training for this position frequently involves on-the-job, hands-on work. Sometimes trainees also attend Damage Controlman School for thirteen weeks. There, students are taught the arts of everything from welding, oxy-fuel gas cutting, and firefighting to carpentry, plumbing, and shipboard damage control.

ELECTRICIAN'S MATE (EM)

Did you ever spend time taking apart the toaster or exploring the inside of a computer tower? That interest in all things electrical will come in handy as an electrician's mate. As an EM, you will not only know which wire goes where and why, but you also will be able to put in new wires and repair old ones. Your most basic mission will be to keep your vessel's electrical systems connected and running at all times, with minimal disruptions at most. EMs install, maintain, repair, and manage very high-tech, state-of-the-art electric and electronic equipment. Specifically, EMs are responsible for maintaining, repairing, and operating:

- Electrical power generators
- Horsepower motors
- Cutter propulsion plants
- Communication systems
- Electronic navigation equipment
- Gyrocompass equipment

An electrician's mate pulls on electrical safety gloves before securing power during a damage control drill on board the coast guard cutter *Bertholf*. This electrician's mate is responsible for securing power to ensure there are no electrical hazards when the fire teams enter affected spaces.

Because EMs cover such a wide variety of jobs and equipment, the training that goes with this position is some of the most intense and thorough in the entire coast guard. In Yorktown, Virginia, you will take classes in everything from mathematics, physics, and electrical component theory to circuit applications and transformer principles. Many of the graduates go on to advanced study in half a dozen specialties. The best guardsmen and women in the field may pursue

JOIN THE FORUM

Want to know more about what members of the coast guard are thinking and talking about? Check out their online forum. There are many different topics listed there, and you can find out all about boot camp, the Coast Guard Academy, life on a coast guard cutter, the work involved, the life of a guardsman or woman, the perks and benefits, the challenges of military service, and much more. Check out the U.S. Coast Guard Forum online at http://www.uscg.org.

two years of college-level courses within the Advanced Computer, Engineering, and Technology education program, resulting in an associate or bachelor's degree.

ELECTRONICS TECHNICIAN (ET)

An electronics technician is like an EM, only with additional and more in-depth training. ETs are in charge of maintaining virtually all of the coast guard's electronics systems, from navigation systems to command, control, communications, and computer (C4) systems. ETs are responsible for the vessel's complex systems, including:

- Command and control systems
- Shipboard weapons
- Guidance and fire control systems
- Communication receivers and transmitters

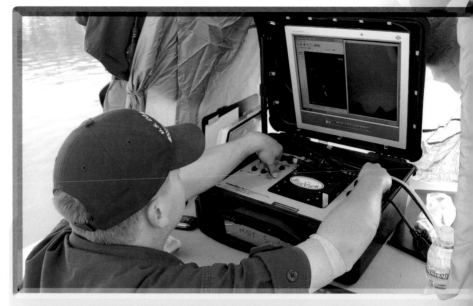

An electronics technician attached to a coast guard Maritime Safety and Security Team controls a remote operating vehicle (ROV). The ROV is an unmanned, highly maneuverable underwater video and data robot used to aid the coast guard with pier sweeps, vessel sweeps, search and recovery, and the detection of improvised explosive devices (IED).

- Data and voice-encryption equipment
- Navigation and search radar
- Tactical and electronic detection systems
- Electronic navigation equipment
- Computers

Training for this field is even more intensive than it is for EMs. Training classes are offered in Petaluma, California, and last for twenty-eight weeks. This includes courses in antenna systems, direction finders, GPS receivers, small boat radar, depth finders, and more. Many ETs go on to a twenty-nine-week Advanced Avionics course or enter the coast guard's two-year Advanced Computer, Engineering, and Technology education program to earn an associate or bachelor's degree.

INFORMATION SYSTEM TECHNICIAN (IT)

No military branch can do its job well if people cannot quickly and efficiently send and receive messages and other vital and sensitive information. Communication is the key to success, and that is where information system technicians, or ITs, are so valuable. Anyone who follows the IT pathway will be in charge of helping people communicate clearly and easily and managing all the information that flows through the coast guard. ITs are responsible for establishing and maintaining coast guard computer systems, analog and digital voice systems (telephones and voice mail), and installing and maintaining the physical network infrastructure that ties the systems together. ITs serving on ships lend support to tactical command, control, communication, and computer systems.

Training for this position includes twenty-five weeks of school in Petaluma, California, where students take classes in how to:

A WALK THROUGH THE MUSEUMS

To learn more about the history of the coast guard, many people like to take a stroll through the Coast Guard Museum, which is on the grounds of the Coast Guard Academy in New London, Connecticut. The museum covers two hundred years of guard history and features models of steamships ranging from two centuries ago to the 270-foot (82.3 m) medium endurance cutter most often used today. Wood carvings of different figureheads are on display, including the one from the training ship *Eagle*.

A second coast guard museum is located in Seattle, Washington. Along with three thousand-plus books and magazines about the coast guard's history, there are also old and new uniforms on display, ship's wheels, ship models, photos, slides, and even a piece of the HMS *Bounty* and "Old Ironsides."

- Maintain computer servers
- Install telephone and network copper and fiber-optic cable
- Perform moves, adds, and changes on private branch exchange and electronic key telephone systems

It is not uncommon for ITs to pursue further education in the coast guard's two-year Advanced Computer, Engineering, and Technology education program.

Machinery Technician (MK)

Calling all gearheads, motor tinkerers, and engine fanatics! The coast guard wants you to serve as a machinery technician. This position is one of the most popular choices for enlisted guardians. MKs work on every coast guard cutter, boat, and shore station. They are expected to be not only mechanics, but also managers and leaders with a thorough understanding and familiarity with:

- Internal combustion engines such as gas or diesel gas turbines
- Environmental support systems such as heating, air-conditioning, and ventilation
- Hydraulics
- Basic electricity
- Hazardous material recovery and control

In addition, many MKs fill the role of federal law enforcement officers. Training for this very important position is provided both on the job and through a twelve-week course in Yorktown, Virginia.

The men and women who choose to pursue hull and engineering jobs are absolutely essential to the smooth functioning of all coast guard vessels and stations. The coast guard cannot begin to perform its many duties without expertly trained personnel who

A seaman, a machinery technician, a boatswain's mate, and a machinery technician apply a jubilee patch to a cracked pipe during a damage-control drill on board the U.S. Coast Guard cutter *Alder*. *Alder* is taking part in Operation Nanook, one of three major operations conducted each year in the Canadian Arctic. The operation is designed to demonstrate international cooperation and expand the international ability to respond to emergencies in the Arctic.

know the vessels and systems inside-out and backward. These are the guardsmen and women who come to the rescue when anything malfunctions, breaks down, wears out, or simply refuses to cooperate.

CHAPTER 5

CAREERS IN AVIATION

I f you thought that the coast guard's fleet of craft included only boats and ships, you are not alone. That is a common misconception. Although it does have 250 cutters (larger than 65 feet, or 20 meters) and 1,872 boats (under 65 feet), it also has a little over two hundred different aircraft. Not only do these planes and helicopters need to be piloted, they also need to be maintained and repaired. The coast guard's avionics department plays an essential part in the service's ability not only to patrol the waterways, but also to respond to search and rescue missions, drug interdictions, and other emergency situations from the air.

AVIONICS ELECTRICAL TECHNICIAN (AET)

When it comes to the typical tasks of AETs, it might be easier to list what they don't do. AETs are trained

An avionics electrical technician pulls the nose of an MH-65C rescue helicopter while a petty officer pushes in preparation for an on-deck rotor head turning evolution aboard the coast guard cutter *Rush*.

to fill all aircrew positions, including navigator, flight mechanic, radio operator, sensor systems operator, and basic air crewman. In addition to all of that, AETs inspect, service, maintain, troubleshoot, and repair the following systems and components of the aircraft:

- Avionics systems that perform communications, navigation, collision avoidance, target acquisition, and automatic flight control functions

- Aircraft batteries
- AC and DC power generation
- Conversion and distribution systems
- Electrical control and indication functions of airframe systems (hydraulics, flight control, landing gear, fuel, environmental control, power plant, drive train, anti-ice and fire detection)

As if this is not enough, AETs also provide routine and regular aircraft repair, maintenance, servicing, and inspections to make sure that everything is working perfectly. Typically, they work on HC-130H (Hercules), HU-25A (Falcon), HH-60J (Jayhawk), and HH-54A (Dolphin) aircraft. AETs are so skilled and essential to the health and well-being of coast guard aircraft that they are described by the service as the coast guard's "aircraft surgeons."

Not surprisingly, the training for this position is intense. It includes classes that teach the concepts required to inspect, service, and maintain aircraft electrical, communication, navigation, auto flight, and sensor systems. Students also study the electrical control and indication functions of all airframe systems, including hydraulics, flight control, landing gear, fuel, environmental control, power plant, drivetrain, anti-ice, and fire detection. AETs are taught how to fabricate and repair cables and wire harnesses, perform corrosion control, and master aviation administrative record keeping.

AVIATION MAINTENANCE TECHNICIAN (AMT)

"AMTs are the MacGyver's of the coast guard," chief aviation maintenance technician and recruiter Russell Kirkham told the author in an interview. "We are the tech guys who know a lot about everything." Like their coworkers, the AETs, the enlisted guardians who choose to become aviation maintenance technicians will have their hands full with almost every aspect of avionics care and maintenance. They are responsible for inspecting, servicing, maintaining, troubleshooting, and repairing:

- Aircraft engines
- Auxiliary power units
- Propellers
- Rotor systems
- Power train systems
- Airframe and systems-specific electrical components
- Aircraft fuselages
- Wings
- Rotor blades
- Flight control surfaces

Petty officers replace the "engine one" starter on an HC-130 Hercules aircraft at the Coast Guard Air Station in Clearwater, Florida. The repaired cargo plane went on to assist in the evacuation of injured people following the devastating earthquakes in Haiti in 2010.

In addition, like AETs, AMTs are expected to fill positions such as flight engineer, flight mechanic, load-master, drop master, sensor systems operator, and basic air crewman. Training occurs over five months and typically takes place at the Aviation Technical Training Center. Some of the enlisted go on to pursue a two-year associate's degree in aeronautical technology.

AVIATION SURVIVAL TECHNICIAN (AST)

If the mechanical side of aircraft appeals to you, but you also have a strong sense of adventure, the AST job might be an excellent choice for you. Unlike the other positions in this division, the AST works with emergency equipment on the aircraft. It is the AST's responsibility to inspect, service, maintain, trouble-shoot, and repair:

- Cargo aerial delivery systems
- Drag parachute systems
- Aircraft oxygen systems
- Helicopter emergency flotation systems
- Portable dewatering pumps
- Air and sea rescue kits
- Special purpose protective clothing
- Storage and handling of aviation ordnance and pyrotechnic devices

INSIDE THE LIVES OF RESCUE SWIMMERS

It may sound exciting to be a coast guard rescue swimmer, but it is an arduous, scary, and dangerous job that requires as much bravery, stamina, and mental toughness as it does swimming ability. More than half of the men and women who qualify for training school do not make it through to graduation. Chief Petty Officer Thor Wentz, who helps run the school, told Doug Sample of the American Forces Press Service, "As far as being difficult, it's extremely difficult. The not truly focused people will tend to disappear in the first couple of days."

Rescue swimmers receive four months of training in how to approach water survivors, as well as how to release and detangle the equipment that might be endangering those trapped in the water. Rescue swimmers must also have basic medical training in order to keep injured survivors alive until they can reach a hospital. "Most people, if they grow up swimming, they become proficient at swimming, but when they are tasked with water duties, that's when we start to see people break down—they begin to panic," explains Wentz. "That's when we say, 'Sorry, you're not right for this program.' Only the mentally tough stick it out."

Mental toughness alone isn't enough, of course. Physical endurance and strength are also essential. The monthly physical training test includes wide-arm push-ups, sit-ups, chin-ups, a twelve-minute crawl swim (500 yards or 457 meters minimum), a 25-yard (23 m) underwater swim, and a 200-yard (183 m) buddy tow. "If you don't have your mind 100 percent, you're not going to make it," Petty Officer 3rd Class Michael Baierski tells Sample. "And if you're not giving 100 percent every single day and pushing yourself as hard as you can, you're going to get kicked out of school."

The instructors are tough, but as Ben Cournia, a rescue swimmer candidate, observed to Sample, "They are not mean, evil people. They get your blood up, but that's what they want to do. You can tell that they really care about how we're doing."

In addition to working with this type of equipment, the AST is frequently put in charge of training others in swim tests and providing land and sea survival classes. Like the other avionics positions, this one requires guardians to fill a number of aircrew positions, including sensor systems operator, drop master or loadmaster on cargo planes, helicopter basic air crewman, and helicopter rescue swimmer. If serving in an aircrew position, the AST may be sent into various rescue missions, including hurricanes, cliff rescues, and emergency medical evacuations from ships at sea.

Initial training involves a four-month AST course that covers aviation life support equipment (ALSE) fundamentals and helicopter rescue swimmer procedures. An AST can then take advanced courses in operational fitness training or become qualified as an emergency medical technician and survival instructor.

A coast guard aviation survival technician (AST) from Coast Guard Air Station Elizabeth City, North Carolina, conducts a man overboard training from a 45-foot (13.7 m) response boat-medium (RB-M).

Although the coast guard relies heavily on its fleet of boats and ships, it also depends greatly on aircraft and the expert technicians who work hard to keep them in perfect shape. Knowing that these machines and all their complex equipment are functioning properly and safely makes it easier to be ready at a moment's notice to head out to life-threatening emergencies and law enforcement actions on the nation's waterways and the high seas. Thanks to the avionics department, coast guard pilots and air crewmen and women can take to the skies with enormous confidence and a high degree of success.

CHAPTER 6

CAREERS IN THE ADMINISTRATIVE AND SCIENTIFIC GROUP

The administrative and scientific group offers some of the most appealing jobs in the coast guard for recruits. Most of the jobs in this group center upon operations support, environmental inspections, and providing care for coast guard personnel. The jobs here often attract those who enjoy working with food, providing health care services, interacting with the public, and harnessing organizational skills. The career paths within the administrative and scientific group include food service specialist, health services technician, marine science technician, public affairs specialist, storekeeper, and yeoman.

FOOD SERVICE SPECIALIST (FS)

Do you like to cook and bake for other people? Is it fun to experiment with new recipes or trot out some tried-and-true old favorites? Do you enjoy the

Students studying to become food service specialists prepare an evening meal at the Coast Guard Training Center in Petaluma, California.

challenge of making meals that are both highly nutritious and incredibly delicious? Or are you interested in acquiring the accounting and management skills necessary to run a successful restaurant? If working in or owning a restaurant sounds fun to you, look into becoming a food service specialist with the coast guard. Not only are food service specialists trained in how to cook and bake for anywhere from dozens to hundreds of people at a time, but they also become skilled in restaurant and culinary accounting, management, leadership, and multitasking. Twelve weeks of classes, plus additional on-the-job training and advanced studies, offer a thorough culinary skills education, including:

- Recipe conversion
- Equipment use and safety

- Basic food preparation skills
- Sanitation
- Purchasing
- Storage
- Nutrition and wellness cooking
- Dining facility management

Regardless of what ship or station you serve, you are guaranteed one thing: all of the enlisted men and women and the officers get hungry, so they will greatly appreciate your talents and creativity. If you happen to do a really outstanding job as an FS, you might even win the coveted Food Service Specialist of the Year award. This award earns recipients two weeks of training at a leading culinary arts school. An FS can even earn certified executive chef credentials during his or her coast guard service.

HEALTH SERVICES TECHNICIAN (HS)

If you have always been interested in helping injured or sick people get better, the position of health services technician might be a wise choice. HS personnel provide a combination of routine health care and emergency services. They help individuals in physical distress and/or in life-threatening situations. They might work in clinics or sick bays, on shore or at sea.

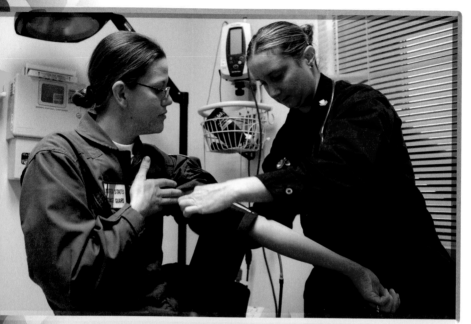

A health services technician wraps a blood pressure cuff around a petty officer's arm. The vital check information includes blood pressure, pulse, and temperature, which is recorded in a member's medical record during every visit to a coast guard clinic.

They work with guardians as well as their families. Some of the job's responsibilities include:

- Assisting medical and dental officers
- Performing diagnostic tests
- Taking X-rays
- Performing clinical lab tests
- Prescribing medications
- Administering immunizations
- Performing minor surgical procedures

Occasionally technicians will also go on search and rescue missions to help provide emergency care to survivors. Training for this position occurs over nineteen weeks in Petaluma, California, where guardians learn about anatomy and physiology; patient examination, evaluation, and treatment; and pharmacology.

MARINE SCIENCE TECHNICIAN (MST)

Marine science technicians are the main servicepeople responsible for fulfilling the coast guard's mission of ensuring maritime protection and safety. This position is ideal for those people who have no trouble switching from one job to another and who do not get stressed by doing something completely different today than they did yesterday and are likely to do tomorrow.

An MST is responsible for many different jobs, depending on the mission he or she is taking part in. These can range from local threats to port security to natural disasters that have national or even international significance. On the water, MSTs inspect containers and patrol harbors. As a domestic vessel examiner, for example, an MST inspects barges, cargo ships, passenger vessels, and gas-carrying vessels to make sure that they are complying with all U.S. laws. MSTs also investigate marine casualties or accidents, as well as pollution incidents. An MST fills the role of

A coast guard senior chief marine science technician *(right)* monitors a controlled fire in the Gulf of Mexico. The U.S. Coast Guard conducted the burn in order to prevent the spread of oil following the 2010 explosion on mobile offshore drilling unit Deepwater Horizon in the Gulf of Mexico.

port state control officer as well. This means that he or she boards a variety of vessels to check that they have safe structural and stability conditions, along with appropriate electrical, fire safety, lifesaving, mechanical, and navigation systems. They also check foreign vessels to ensure that proper living standards are being maintained for crew members. MSTs examine harbor facilities to ensure that the proper environmental response equipment and procedures are in place and available. In advance of all of these types of missions, an MST is expected to plan each step and see that everything is carried out safely and properly.

Training for this very important position begins with eight weeks of instruction in Yorktown, Pennsylvania. Students receive instruction in the following areas:

- Investigating oil and hazardous material pollution incidents
- Supervising pollution cleanup operations
- Performing waterfront facility and security inspections
- Conducting safety and security boardings on foreign registered vessels coming into the territorial waters of the country

MSTs need to be able to learn a great deal about many different roles and be prepared to switch from one to the other whenever necessary and at a moment's notice.

PUBLIC AFFAIRS SPECIALIST (PA)

If you've ever given any thought to being a journalist, writer, photographer, Web designer, videographer/filmmaker, spokesperson, or media rep, the position of public affairs specialist will most likely appeal to you. In this job, you are the liaison between the public and the coast guard. You will write news releases for radio, television, and the Internet, as well as feature articles and

ANOTHER COAST GUARD FIRST

On April 9, 2010, Lieutenant Jeanine Menze had a particularly pleasant job to perform. As the first African American female aviator in the U.S. Coast Guard, she was given the chance to pin a set of wings on Lieutenant La'Shanda Holmes, the first African American helicopter pilot in the coast guard. Although there are approximately 1,200 pilots in the coast guard, only about 85 are female. Holmes is currently stationed at the Air Station in Los Angeles, California, and looks forward to protecting her country's borders and helping those in peril. She is also eager to inspire other young women. "When I think of my sisters [and other young women] and the journey that they are about to begin," she tells the African American news Web site The Grio, "I know that I have to live to a higher standard for them. Young people are constantly watching and listening, even when we think they aren't. I don't ever want them to stop looking at me with those wide eyes burning with inspiration and hope."

public speeches. You will shoot still and video imagery and work to keep all print and online material regarding the coast guard both accurate and up to date.

Training for this position includes a twelve-week course in Fort Meade, Maryland, at the Defense Information School. After this coursework is completed, you have the option of going into specific fields, such as:

- Photojournalism
- Digital imagery
- Editing and design
- Media relations
- Crisis communications

A public affairs specialist stationed in Jacksonville, Florida, speaks to the media regarding a successful search and rescue mission.

If being in front of or behind the camera appeals to you, you have a strong public speaking ability and good writing skills, and you exhibit grace under pressure, this creative position might be just right for you.

STOREKEEPER (SK)

Do you like crunching numbers and balancing accounts? Have you always been good at managing your money earned from allowance, odd jobs, and after-school employment? Are you comfortable keeping inventory lists—for example, of items in the pantry that are on hand and items that are lacking and need to be purchased—and checking them twice? Explore the coast guard position of storekeeper. Believe it or not, it is considered one of the most important enlisted jobs in the coast guard. The SK is the person who always makes sure there is enough of every item needed by all the other guardians and officers, including clothes, spare parts, reading material, and provisions (food and drink, soap, toothpaste, shampoo, batteries, and other necessities).

In order to do this, SKs keep inventories, prepare requisitions, and check all incoming supplies so that they know how much they have of everything in the store and what needs to be ordered and restocked. They also learn the coast guard's accounting system so that they can prepare financial reports. They operate forklifts and other types of material-handling equipment on a regular basis.

Training for this position involves a seven-week, performance-based course in which participants actually perform the tasks of an SK. Practical exercises during this course include hands-on learning of:

- The coast guard accounting system
- The coast guard message system
- The researching of federal logistics data
- The use of messaging, finance, and procurement systems and software
- Fiscal procedures
- Shipping and receiving
- Inventory management
- Property management
- Transportation of freight

KEEPING UP WITH THE COAST GUARD ONLINE

If you want to see the latest photos, videos, and news reports regarding the coast guard and its current activities and missions, check out the Coast Guard Headquarters' Media Port online at https://www.piersystem.com/go/doc/786/440291. This gives you a chance to observe close-up what kinds of missions the guardians go on and what kinds of jobs they perform. Another way to keep up to date with the coast guard is through its official Facebook page. It can be found at http://www.facebook.com/UScoastguard. To see an overview of coast guard activity during the previous year, go to the latest issue of *Coast Guard Outlook*, found online at https://www.piersystem.com/external/content/document/786/977991/1/CG%20Outlook%202011%20Printed%20Publication.pdf. *Coast Guard Outlook* is an official coast guard magazine and outlines the service's current plans, programs, and budgetary needs. Lastly, read the coast guard's official blog, the Coast Guard Compass, at http://coastguard.dodlive.mil. The coast guard can also be found on YouTube, Flickr, and Twitter.

The SK is the person everyone will go to when they need something right away. So an ability to recognize an item by name, locate it quickly, and provide it will make you many friends in the coast guard and advance your career!

YEOMAN (YN)

According to the coast guard, yeomans are problem solvers, counselors, and human resource managers all rolled up into one. They are the answer people—if you have a question, they either know the answer or know where to find it. Often, YNs provide vital information to guardsmen and women concerning career choices or career moves, promotions, education and advanced training options, incentive programs, veterans' benefits, and retirement options. Training to become a YN involves a six-week course in Petaluma, California, on-the-job training, or a distance learning online course.

The administrative and scientific group is made up of the behind-the-scenes people who keep everything running. They feed, clothe, counsel, and care for the guardsmen and women. Without them, the coast guard would quickly grind to a halt!

CHAPTER 7

CAREERS IN OFFICERS' PROGRAMS

Have you thought about entering the coast guard as an officer, rather than as an enlisted? In many ways, this makes good sense. Officers qualify for higher paychecks. They have the more advanced jobs, and they enjoy greater authority, respect, and perks. Also, according to the new edition of *The Armed Forces Officer*, published by the U.S. Department of Defense, being a member of the officer class carries a great deal of pride and personal and professional satisfaction. The book states,

As an officer in the armed forces of the United States, you are a warrior in the profession of arms, a leader of character, an unwavering defender of the Constitution, a servant of the nation, and an exemplar and champion of its ideals. You accept unmitigated personal responsibility and accountability to duty, for your actions and those of your subordinates. In so doing, you willingly take your place in an ancient and honorable calling, obligated equally to those who have gone before you, those you walk among, and those who will follow.

AREAS OF SPECIALIZATION

Officers can specialize in many different fields, including:

FIELD	GENERAL DEFINITION	POSSIBLE SPECIALTIES	DEGREE REQUIRED
Aviation	Conducting long-range patrols in fixed-wing aircraft, piloting helicopters in search and rescue missions, and flying high-speed jets to intercept drug smugglers.		General college degree
Command, control, communications, and computers (C4)	Specifying, procuring, implementing, testing, validating, configuring, maintaining, and managing computer and information systems and computer networks. Responsibilities include database administration, systems analysis and design, network design and administration, systems integration, and computer system management.	Electrical engineering, computer and information system management, and telecommunications management.	Computer science or information systems; electrical engineering
Engineering logistics	Engineering jobs include supporting long- and short-range help in navigation and working with engineering plants.	Naval engineering; civil engineering; ocean engineering; industrial management; command, control, and communications; and aeronautical engineering	Engineering or the sciences

FIELD	GENERAL DEFINITION	POSSIBLE SPECIALTIES	DEGREE REQUIRED
Civil engineering	Managing coast guard shore plants by planning, programming, budgeting, designing, constructing, operating, maintaining, and managing the environment		Civil engineering or allied field
Naval engineering	Planning, designing, constructing, outfitting, operating, maintaining, and altering automated machinery and electrical and ordnance systems for more than 30,000 buildings and roads, lighthouses, runways, etc.		Engineering or related technical field
Financial resource management	Performing as everything from district budget officer to commanding officer at the CG Finance Center	Comptroller, financial management, fiscal operation, supply and inventory management, supply operations, and contracting and resale programs	Advanced finance
Human resources management	Managing people flows; human performance technology, education, and training; career and personal development; and support services in housing, benefits, compensation, and medical care	Human resource management, recruiting, training, systems and services, medical administration, and reserve programs	Related to the field
Health services	Providing health care to guardians, dependents, and retirees	USPHS officers (doctors, dentists, pharmacists, etc.), medical administration officers, and physician assistants	Medical (in some cases)

FIELD	GENERAL DEFINITION	POSSIBLE SPECIALTIES	DEGREE REQUIRED
Legal	Providing a wide variety of law services to guardians, officers, and families	Claims and litigation, environmental law, maritime and international law, legislation, regulatory and administrative law, procurement law, military justice, general law, legal assistance, and direct commission lawyers	Law
Maritime safety	Supporting pollution prevention and response, performing marine inspections and investigations, providing marine licensing, and managing waterways	Commercial vessel safety, port safety and security, and marine environmental protection	Naval architecture, marine engineering, or hazardous materials (not always required)
Operations (afloat, ashore, law enforcement, intelligence)	Assisting in operations of all types of missions and in all environments	Afloat: law enforcement, search and rescue, defense operations, aids to navigation and ice operations (polar operations and domestic icebreaking). Ashore: search and rescue planning and management, command, and support; research and development. Intelligence: collection, analysis, and dissemination of information. Law enforcement: drug interdiction, fisheries enforcement, and alien migrant interdiction	Varies with assignment

BECOMING A COAST GUARD OFFICER

There are several ways for you to become a coast guard officer and several different officer programs available to people. They include:

- The Coast Guard Academy
- The College Student Pre-Commissioning Initiative (Scholarship Program)
- Officer Candidate School
- Direct Commission Program

The Coast Guard Academy

Located in New London, Connecticut, the Coast Guard Academy states that its mission is "to produce leaders of character for service to the nation." Each year, approximately three hundred high school graduates enroll here. Four years later, they graduate with a bachelor of science degree and the coast guard position of ensign. Tuition is free, and students are given a modest paycheck during their studies. About 70 percent of the students graduate with a technical degree in areas such as:

- Civil engineering
- Mechanical engineering
- Naval architecture
- Marine engineering

A color guard passes in front of Hamilton Hall at the Coast Guard Academy in New London, Connecticut.

- Electrical engineering
- Operations research and computer analysis
- Marine environmental science

After graduating, cadets are expected to serve in the coast guard for five years. Applications are accepted online, and the annual deadline is February 1. In 2010, 1,030 cadets were enrolled, representing more than 40 states. Almost 30 percent were women, and 17 percent were minorities. Everyone lives on campus, and there are more than twenty athletic teams men and women can join. The average class size is nineteen cadets, and there is an average of one faculty member for every eight students.

Wonder what it is like to live at the academy? Here is a typical day's schedule for cadets:

TIME	EVENT
6:00 AM	Reveille [wake-up]
6:20	Morning formation/breakfast
7:00	Military training period
8:00	Academic day begins
12:05 PM	Noon formation/lunch
1:00	Afternoon classes begin
3:40	End of academic day
4:00–6:00	Athletic period
5:00–7:00	Evening meal
7:00	Military training period/activity hour
8:00–10:00	Evening study hour
10:00	Taps (lights out)

Players from the U.S. Coast Guard Academy Bears run onto the football field while surrounded by their fellow cadets at the Coast Guard Academy in New London, Connecticut. The Coast Guard Bears played their rivals from the Merchant Marine Academy in a game known as the Secretary's Cup.

The weekends are quite similar, except you get to sleep in a little later. On Saturdays, cadets are free to do as they please after 1:00 in the afternoon. On Sundays, church attendance is required in the morning, but afternoons are free until the dinner meal at 5:00.

COLLEGE STUDENT PRE-COMMISSIONING INITIATIVE (SCHOLARSHIP PROGRAM)

This coast guard program is designed for college sophomores and juniors. Their last two years of college are paid for by the coast guard, including school tuition, fees, textbooks, medical insurance, and even a salary. After being accepted into the program, recruits have two years to complete their degrees. They are then sent to the Officer Candidate School to be commissioned as officers. After that, they are committed to three years of active duty. College students who would like to be part of this program must submit their packet of information by the annual deadline of January 10.

OFFICER CANDIDATE SCHOOL

At the coast guard's Officer Candidate School, college graduates who can pass certain eligibility requirements are trained for seventeen weeks on how to serve as effective coast guard officers. Graduates are given the rank of ensign and must serve three years of active duty. Eligibility requirements include:

- Candidates must be between the ages of twenty-one and thirty-four.
- Candidates must have U.S. citizenship.

An officer in training *(left)* gets navigation advice from a local boat pilot while transiting into port in Portsmouth, New Hampshire. She is participating in the College Student Pre-Commissioning Initiative, which pays for her final two years of college in exchange for three years active-duty service as a commissioned officer.

- Minimum test scores of 1,100 (combined verbal and math) on the SAT, 23 on the ACT, and 109 on the ASVAB General Technical Aptitude Area.
- Baccalaureate or higher degree from an accredited college or university, or 25th percentile on general CLEP exams, or completion of at least one year of college.

DIRECT COMMISSION PROGRAM

This coast guard program is designed for those who are already professional lawyers, aviators, engineers, environmental specialists, or former military officers. These people are eligible to become officers without having to go to Officer Candidate School or through boot camp. Typically, they must be U.S. citizens between the ages of twenty-one and thirty four, and meet standard physical requirements.

A WORD FROM COAST GUARD COMMANDANT ADMIRAL ROBERT J. PAPP

In Admiral Robert J. Papp's State of the Coast Guard address, he explained why the coast guard was so important to the country. He stated:

The coast guard is a unique instrument of national power, which we demonstrate in a range of duties from our national security and law enforcement mission to promoting boating safety on federal waterways. We are an effective and efficient organization, from the tactical to the strategic level, using risk-based decision-making to ensure that our nation is best served. We are also an agency that practices a principle of on-scene initiative—seniors trust juniors to do the right thing "on scene" once an objective and a course of action are developed. By empowering the coxswain on scene or the aircraft commander deploying a rescue swimmer, we streamline our operations and perform in a matter that promotes mission accomplishment. This is a true value.

Let's take a closer look at each position made available through this program.

Direct commission aviators are what the coast guard calls their "poster jobs." These pilots are involved in virtually every mission area. The qualifications for this position include being a graduate of a U.S. military flight training program and having flight experience within two years of application.

A direct commission engineer position is for those who want to work with the design, construction, and maintenance of all coast guard vessels and the service's electronics, communication systems, and information systems. These engineers also design systems to prevent oil spills.

The Direct Commission Intelligence Officers division has grown a great deal since the coast guard became part of the U.S. Department of Homeland Security. Intelligence professionals who have already been working in the field and have received high security clearance for working with sensitive information often choose this path to officer status. They are given an additional three- to five-week training course, which includes a program designed to acclimate them to life in the military and ease their transition from the civilian world into the coast guard.

Civilian lawyers are accepted into the coast guard's Direct Commission Program to work in these general legal practice areas: criminal law/military justice,

Members of Officer Candidate School prepare for a drill-down competition at the U.S. Coast Guard Academy.

operations, international activities, civil advocacy, environmental law, internal organizational law, regulations and administrative law, legislative support, and legal assistance. This means they apply their legal know-how and experience to everything from helping an officer with retirement and estate planning to investigating marine casualties to protecting national security issues.

To learn more details about being an officer in the coast guard, read the *Career Development Guidebook*, available online at http://www.uscg.mil/ hq/capemay/education/doc/OCareerDevGuidebook. pdf. It can answer every question you have about the pros and cons of joining the coast guard as an officer, rather than as an enlisted guardian.

CHAPTER 8

PERSONAL AND PROFESSIONAL LIFE AFTER THE COAST GUARD

No matter which career pathway you choose to follow within the coast guard, you will eventually reach the end of your contract. It will then be time either to re-enlist or to leave the military life behind you and return to the civilian world. This is a decision not to be taken lightly and can often be quite agonizing. For this reason, the coast guard offers transition guidance and support to its officers to help clarify the decision-making process and make the transition into civilian life smoother and easier. In addition, the U.S. Department of Labor created the Transition Assistance Program (TAP) to help every military member from any of the armed forces successfully make the shift back into civilian life. TAP offers free reading materials and workshops on topics ranging from assessing your professional skills to acing a job interview. These materials can be found for free online at http://images.military.com/transition/tap1_2.pdf.

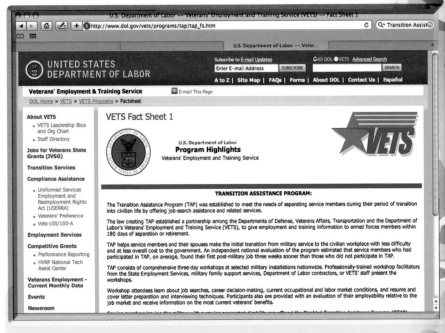

Information on the employment and training possibilities available to veterans, as well as assistance in transitioning from military to civilian life, can be found at the U.S. Department of Labor's Web site (http://www.dol.gov/vets).

Many employers are happy to hire former military members. They recognize that these men and women have had excellent training and schooling and have acquired the habit of self-discipline, hard work, and dedication through years of excellent service in the armed forces. All of these qualities make for a superior employee and help former coast guard members stand out from the pack of fellow competitors for a job.

When you are preparing to make the transition, TAP recommends that you create a portfolio or packet of information for presentation to a potential employer. Recommended paperwork to include in it are a résumé, a list of professional and character references (with contact information), military service papers (training records, honors and awards, and service record), a list of work experience (history, honors/citations, community involvement, and references), and your education and training outside of the military (transcripts, diplomas, honors, and certifications).

DECK AND ORDNANCE– RELATED CAREERS IN THE CIVILIAN WORLD

One of the biggest benefits to joining any military branch, including the coast guard, is that you get a strong, solid education in any number of fields. Every bit of training you get, either as an enlisted guardian or as an officer, can be readily transferred to jobs in the civilian world. Remember all the jobs you read about in previous chapters? Let's revisit those again to see how they correlate to civilian jobs. In the Deck and Ordnance group, for example, here are the coast guard jobs paired with comparable careers in the civilian world:

A machinery technician and member of the Maritime Safety and Security Team keeps an eye out for any trouble in New York Harbor near the Statue of Liberty on December 22, 2003. The coast guard increases patrols whenever the national security threat level is raised.

COAST GUARD JOB	CIVILIAN JOBS
Boatswain's mate	Pier superintendent, tugboat crew-man, heavy equipment operator or supervisor, ship pilot
Gunner's mate	Small arms trainer, electronics mechanic, armorer/gunsmith, ammunition foreman, hydraulic equipment operator, mechanic
Intelligence specialist	Intelligence analyst, manager, or collector; counterintelligence specialist; counterterrorism specialist; joint ops coordinator

COAST GUARD JOB	CIVILIAN JOBS
Operations specialist	City/county/state emergency operations coordinator
Maritime enforcement specialist	Local, state, or federal law enforcement; physical and personal security positions

HULL AND ENGINEERING–RELATED CAREERS IN THE CIVILIAN WORLD

In the hull and engineering job group, there were five jobs to choose from. Let's see how they translate into civilian work.

COAST GUARD JOB	CIVILIAN JOBS
Damage controlman	Welder, plumber, carpenter, pipe pitter, ship fitter, firefighter, home or building inspector, trade school teacher, construction foreman, maintenance supervisor
Electrician's mate	Industrial plant technician, generating plant technician, industrial electrician, shipyard electrician, electrical field service technician, power and instrumentation technician, facilities technician, electrical maintenance technician
Electronics technician	Electronics technician; guidance systems specialist; radio, TV, and radar repair; computer technician; electronics installation technician (cable TV, satellite); technical writer; data communications specialist

THE COAST GUARD UNIFORM

In the coast guard, there are three types of uniforms: the operational dress uniform, tropical blues, and service dress blues. The operational dress uniform is the daily uniform and the most commonly seen. It is all the same shade of blue. Starting at the top, it includes a ball cap, a crew neck T-shirt, and an over-shirt (button-up), with the nametape above the right pocket and the U.S. Coast Guard patch above the left pocket. The pants are matching blue and tucked into black safety boots. A black belt is also required. Occasionally a jacket, foul-weather coat, or parka is added for outerwear.

Tropical blues are worn in areas where it is unusually warm and the standard uniform would be too hot. It includes a short-sleeve, light-blue shirt, complete with ribbons, name tag, and appropriate insignias. A black belt with brass buckle is required, along with black dress shoes. Women are allowed a blue skirt, and, in cooler weather, a cardigan, windbreaker, trench coat, or parka is permitted.

Finally, service dress blues are worn on formal and ceremonial occasions. A dress shirt is matched with a blue tie for men and blue tie tab for women. The jacket has medals, ribbons, and name tag on it. A black belt is standard, along with black socks and oxford shoes.

COAST GUARD JOB	CIVILIAN JOBS
Information system technician	Telephone technician, network technician, computer systems technician, voice and data technician, telecommunications technician, central office technician
Machinery technician	Auto/truck mechanic; heavy-duty equipment repair; heating, ventilation, and air-conditioning; shipyard work

ADMINISTRATIVE AND SCIENTIFIC–RELATED CAREERS IN THE CIVILIAN WORLD

Are you beginning to see how the skills and training you have learned on the job while serving in the coast guard can translate into careers in the civilian world? Every single skill you acquire in the coast guard can be applied in the civilian job market.

In the coast guard's administrative and scientific group of jobs, all six positions translate well into civilian employment.

COAST GUARD JOB	CIVILIAN JOBS
Food service specialist	Chef, restaurant manager, caterer, baker, cook
Health services technician	Medical assistant, X-ray technician, medical laboratory technician, physician assistant

A marine science technician and field observer in Cocodrie, Lousiana, recovers an oiled pelican from the water near Racoon Island following the explosion of the Deepwater Horizon offshore oil rig in 2010. The pelican was shipped to a bird rehabilitation center, where it was treated and prepared for return into the wild.

COAST GUARD JOB	CIVILIAN JOBS
Marine science technician	Marine environmental specialist, marine safety specialist, hazardous materials specialist, oil and hazardous spill responder, facility supervisor, vessel inspector, OSHA response trainer
Public affairs specialist	Public relations, news reporter, Web designer, freelance writer, videographer, professional photographer, desktop publishing designer

COAST GUARD JOB	CIVILIAN JOBS
Storekeeper	Inventory manager, purchaser, accountant, bookkeeper, shipping and receiving clerk, warehouse supervisor, logistics specialist
Yeoman	Human resources specialist, executive assistant, personnel manager, administrative assistant

AVIATION-RELATED CAREERS IN THE CIVILIAN WORLD

Remember the jobs that fell under the general heading of aviation in an earlier chapter? Let's see how they can transition to the civilian world.

COAST GUARD JOB	CIVILIAN JOBS
Aviation maintenance technician	Flight engineer, airline maintenance supervisor, general/commercial aviation mechanic, general/commercial aircraft inspector, aviation maintenance instructor, aircraft ground handler
Aviation survival technician	Commercial aircraft life support equipment technician, aircraft ground handler, parachute rigging and repair, emergency medical technician, land and water survival instructor, aviation maintenance instructor, aircraft mechanic, supply technician, quality insurance inspector

COAST GUARD JOB	CIVILIAN JOBS
Avionics electrical technician	Aircraft electrician, ground handler, avionics technician or instructor, general/ commercial aircraft avionics inspector

OTHER STEPS TO TAKE

Along with your résumé, a list of professional and character references, and portfolio of professional skills and accomplishments, what else should you prepare as you think about applying for jobs? Make a list of your strengths. There are more of them than you may think. Life in the military teaches you numerous skills outside of the classroom, such as leadership, obedience, discipline, teamwork, punctuality, follow-through, safety, and organization. All of these are invaluable skills that employers love to see in the workplace. TAP offers a worksheet of over fifty skill areas that might apply to you, so check it out.

TAP has quite a bit of advice regarding the job search and interview process, including asking yourself questions in order to identify your work preferences, analyzing your work-related values, and assessing your financial needs. In addition, it provides a list of places to look for jobs, such as:

- Business magazines
- Business sections of newspapers

AN AVERAGE DAY IN THE COAST GUARD

According to the 2010 issue of *The Coast Guard Outlook*, the following took place on an average day in the coast guard that year.

- Thirteen lives were saved.
- Sixty-four search and rescue cases were responded to.
- Seventy-seven percent of mariners in imminent danger were rescued.
- Nine hundred and fifty-nine pounds (435 kg) of cocaine were seized and prevented from hitting the streets.
- $260,000 in property was protected.
- Ten undocumented migrants were stopped from entering the United States.
- Sixty buoys were either repaired or serviced.
- Six hundred and seventy-nine commercial vessels and 170,000 crew and passengers were screened.
- Seventy containers were inspected.
- Twelve marine accidents were investigated.
- Thirty-three vessels were inspected for compliance with pollution standards.
- Fifteen fishing boats were boarded to ensure compliance with fishing laws.
- Ten pollution accidents were investigated.
- Four U.S. Navy vessels were escorted safely through U.S. waterways.

- One person with terrorist associations was identified.
- Six patrol boats and four hundred guardians protected Iraq's offshore oil infrastructure, trained Iraqi naval forces, and kept sea lanes secure in the Arabian Gulf.

Not bad for an average day's work!

- Chambers of commerce
- Colleges/universities
- Employment agencies, services, and counselors
- Internet
- Internships
- Job fairs and job shares
- Library research
- Occupational handbooks
- Contacts: Family, friends, teachers, personal acquaintances
- Trade shows
- Training and apprenticeship programs
- Volunteer organizations

TAP also offers advice on how to write effective cover letters and resumes, how to analyze job ads to find those most suitable to your experience and qualifications, and the best, most professional ways to respond to both being turned down for a job and receiving a job offer.

OFFICER TRANSITIONS

The coast guard's human resources department offers a special program of preparation counseling for officers who are leaving the service. This program covers everything from employment and relocation assistance to information on education, training, and benefits. Though designed for officers, much of this can be adapted for use by enlisted guardians as well.

The program begins with helping each person develop an individual transition plan. They divide this up into seven phases. Each phase is broken down into important steps and questions.

Phase 1: Self-Assessment

Ask and answer these questions:

- What positions have you held?
- What are your interests?
- What are your needs and wants?
- What subject matter and style of learning do you prefer?
- What are your personality traits and physical capabilities?
- What is important to you?

A resident is rescued from the rooftop of a home by the U.S. Coast Guard as floodwaters from Hurricane Katrina cover the streets of New Orleans, Louisiana.

Phase 2: Exploration

The steps of phase 2 include:

- List jobs and careers that appeal to you and meet your parameters.
- Research careers, companies, salaries, and benefits.
- Identify required skills.

Phase 3: Skills Development

Develop the skills you need, and consider utilizing support services such as:

- Educational assistance
- Small business administration
- Interest inventories
- Financial planning
- Disability benefits
- Relocation assistance

Phase 4: Trial Programs

See if there are any opportunities for you to take part in internships, volunteer jobs, temporary services, or even part-time jobs to see what you enjoy the most. There is always the chance that a part-time job or internship can lead to permanent employment.

Phase 5: Job Search

This phase involves the process of setting goals, preparing a résumé, networking to develop leads, and practicing interview skills. Seeking employment is in itself a full-time job. One must apply oneself to the effort all day, every day.

Phase 6: Job Selection

Experts do not recommend accepting the first job you are offered. Instead, wait and weigh your options to find the best fit.

Phase 7: Support

This last aspect of the transition process focuses on tying up loose ends. Finish the relocation process, reorganize your paperwork and finances, and manage your stress levels at this often anxious time of uncertainty and transition.

Making the transition from the coast guard to civilian life is also easier with support. So be sure to check out Turbo TAP (http://www.turbotap.org), the official Department of Defense Web site established to help members of the military smoothly shift into life in the nonmilitary world. This site provides information on everything from health care and insurance issues to veteran's and disability benefits.

Coast guardsmen aboard a response boat enforce a safety zone around these swimming wild horses at the 83rd Annual Pony Swim in Chincoteague, Virginia. The U.S. Coast Guard, U.S. Coast Guard Auxiliary, and Virginia Marine Resources Commission were all present to enforce safety laws regarding life jackets, licenses, no-wake zones, and safety perimeters.

THE AUXILIARY

If leaving the coast guard seems like too drastic a move for you, you might consider joining the U.S. Coast Guard Auxiliary. It is made up of a group of volunteers across the country who help their communities by teaching recreational boating safety and and marine safety. It has been in place since 1939. During World War II, more than fifty thousand auxiliary coast guard members helped to monitor waterfronts, carry out coastal patrols, rescue survivors from ships, and provide any other maritime-related service that was required.

Today, tens of thousands of men and women volunteer millions of hours every year to help teach others about how to stay safe on the water. They also offer free examinations to help people make sure their recreational boats meet federal boating regulations. Along with these responsibilities, the auxiliary assists with search and rescue missions, mobilization exercises, harbor and pollution patrols, and coast guard recruiting. The auxiliary has members in all fifty states, as well as Puerto Rico, the Virgin Islands, American Samoa, and Guam. Anyone age seventeen and up is welcome— whether a coast guard alumni or not. Leaving the coast guard can be very difficult because guardians cherish their experiences, bond with their fellow sailors, and derive enormous satisfaction from their work and sense of mission. Luckily, guardians have lots of options. They can serve in the coast guard all their lives and advance their military careers. They can depart from the coast guard and parlay the education and skills they gained in the service into successful civilian careers. Or they can choose a middle way—continuing to serve in the reserves or as an auxiliary while pursuing a career in the civilian world. There are no bad options when it comes to service in the coast guard. Rather, there are nothing but special opportunities and invaluable experiences.

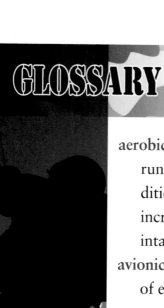

GLOSSARY

aerobic Involving exercise, such as running or swimming, that conditions the heart and lungs by increasing the efficiency of oxygen intake by the body.

avionics The science and technology of electronic systems and devices as applied to aeronautics.

civilian A person who is not on active duty with a military organization.

conscientious objector Someone who refuses to serve in the armed forces on moral grounds, in opposition to a particular conflict, because of a belief in pacifism, or for reasons of personal conscience.

coxswain A petty officer or other person in charge of a ship's boat and acting as its steersman; the helmsman of a ship.

culinary Relating to or used in cooking or the kitchen.

cutter A ship that is typically more than 65 feet (20 m) long.

debriefing The receiving of information or a report concerning a just completed mission or task.

decontamination The removal of contaminants or toxins.

dependents Minors or those who are financially dependent upon someone.

enlisted Someone who is voluntarily enrolled in the military.

fiscal Pertaining to financial matters.

hoist To raise or haul up, often with the help of a mechanical device.

integrity Sound moral principles; uprightness, honesty, and sincerity.

interdiction The interception of illegal drugs or migrants while being smuggled in by air, land, or sea.

liaison A means of communication between different groups or units of an organization; a linking up or connecting of the various parts of a whole in order to achieve better communication and coordination of activities.

maritime Relating to or involving ships, navigation, shipping, sailors, or the sea; nautical.

migrant A person who moves from one region to another, usually in search of work and a better life.

ordnance Cannon or artillery; all military weapons, including ammunition, combat vehicles, and the equipment and supplies used in servicing them; the branch of the military that orders, stores, and issues weapons, combat vehicles, and ammunition.

pyrotechnics Fireworks or other kinds of light displays; any devices or materials that activate propellants, safety systems, or signals by igniting or exploding on command.

requisition An authoritative, formal, often written request or demand; often the request is for equipment, tools, food, or services.

stewardship Being in charge of and responsible for something and the tasks associated with it; serving as a supervisor or administrator over something; guiding, guarding, and nurturing that which is in your charge.

FOR MORE INFORMATION

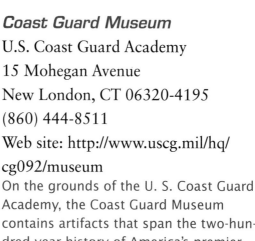

Coast Guard Museum
U.S. Coast Guard Academy
15 Mohegan Avenue
New London, CT 06320-4195
(860) 444-8511
Web site: http://www.uscg.mil/hq/
cg092/museum

On the grounds of the U. S. Coast Guard Academy, the Coast Guard Museum contains artifacts that span the two-hundred-year history of America's premier maritime service. Featuring everything from models of a series of early steamships to the 270-foot (82 m) cutter that plies the waters today, the craftsmanship captures the changes in ship design over the last two hundred years. Other fascinating objects include 10-foot-tall (3 m) lighthouse lenses, ship figureheads, cannons, paintings, uniforms, and medals. The grounds also offer visitors the opportunity to watch flag raising and lowering, attend coast guard chapel services, board the coast guard ship *Eagle*, and observe cadets at work and taking part in drills. Visitors are immersed in the history of the U.S. Coast Guard and its predecessors: the Life Saving Service, the Steamboat Inspection Service, the Lighthouse Establishment, and the Revenue Cutter Service.

Coast Guard Museum Northwest

Pier 36, Base Seattle

1519 Alaskan Way South

Seattle, WA 98134

(206) 217-6993

Web site: http://www.rexmwess.com/cgpatchs/cogard-museum.html

The Coast Guard Museum Northwest includes thousands of coast guard–related items, such as a Lighthouse Service clock, circa 1860; uniforms, old and new; ship's wheels and binnacles; a number of lighthouse and buoy lenses; a piece of HMS *Bounty*; part of the USS *Constitution* ("Old Ironsides"); the coast guard flag carried on the first space shuttle flight; several large models of Revenue Cutter Service and coast guard cutters; the ship's bell from the steam tug *Roosevelt*, Admiral Peary's ship during his quest for the North Pole; thousands of photos and slides of cutter, aircraft, lighthouses, crews, and stations; and the largest public collection of coast guard patches.

National Maritime Center

100 Forbes Drive

Martinsburg, WV 25404

(888) I-ASK-NMC (427-5662)

Web site: http://www.uscg.mil/nmc

The National Maritime Center is the licensing authority for the U.S. Coast Guard under the auspices of the Department of Homeland Security. Its mission is to issue credentials to fully qualified mariners in the most effective and efficient manner possible in order to assure a safe, secure, economically efficient, and environmentally sound Marine Transportation System.

U.S. Coast Guard Academy

15 Mohegan Avenue
New London, CT 06320-4195
(800) 883-8724
Web site: http://www.cga.edu
The U.S. Coast Guard Academy's Web site helps you understand what life is like at the academy, from classes and standard schedules to instructors and the morals and values of the coast guard.

U.S. Coast Guard Headquarters

2100 2nd Street SW
Washington, DC 20593
(202) 372-4600
Web site: http://www.uscg.mil
The U.S. Coast Guard is one of the five armed forces of the United States and the only military organization within the Department of Homeland Security. The coast guard protects the maritime economy and the environment, defends America's maritime borders, and saves those in peril.

U.S. Coast Guard Navigation Center

NAVCEN 7310
7323 Telegraph Road
Alexandria, VA 20598
(703) 313-5900
Web site: http://www.navcen.uscg.gov
The U.S. Coast Guard Navigation Center's Web site is sponsored by the U.S. Department of Homeland Security. It provides up-to-date news stories about coast guard

missions, as well as maritime information and other navigation points of interest.

U.S. Coast Guard Recruiting

2300 Wilson Boulevard, Suite 500

Arlington, VA 20598-7500

(877) 669-8724

Web site: http://www.gocoastguard.com

The U.S. Coast Guard Recruiting's Web site provides
everything you need to know about the coast guard and
features videos highlighting each kind of job within the
organization. It connects you with recruiters and has a
thorough FAQ section.

WEB SITES

Due to the changing nature of Internet links, Rosen
Publishing has developed an online list of Web sites
related to the subject of this book. This site is updated
regularly. Please use this link to access the list:

http://www.rosenlinks.com/cod/cgrd

FOR FURTHER READING

Beard, Tom. *The Coast Guard*. New York, NY: Universe, 2010.

Benson, Michael. *The U.S. Coast Guard*. Minneapolis, MN: Lerner Classroom, 2005.

Braulick, Carrie. *The U.S. Coast Guard*. Mankato, MN: Capstone Press, 2005.

Braulick, Carrie. *U.S. Coast Guard Cutters*. Mankato, MN: Capstone Press, 2006.

Caldwell, Francis. *The Search for the Amigo*. Bloomington, IN: Trafford Publishing, 2006.

de Quesada, Alejandro. *U.S. Coast Guard in World War II*. Botley, England: Osprey Publishing, 2010.

Dolan, Edward. *Careers in the U.S. Coast Guard*. Salt Lake City, UT: Benchmark Books, 2009.

Frump, Robert. *Two Tankers Down: The Greatest Small-Boat Rescue in U.S. Coast Guard History*. Guilford, CT: The Lyons Press, 2008.

Goldish, Meish. *Coast Guard: Civilian to Guardian.* New York, NY: Bearport Publishing, 2010.

Hamilton, John. *The Coast Guard* (Defending the Nation). Edina, MN: Checkerboard Books, 2007.

Helvarg, David. *Rescue Warriors: The U.S. Coast Guard, America's Forgotten Heroes.* New York, NY: Thomas Dunne Books, 2009.

Hoover, Gerald R. *Brotherhood of the Fin: A Coast Guard Rescue Swimmer's Story.* Tucson, AZ: Wheatmark, 2007.

Kroll, C. Douglas. *A Coast Guardsman's History of the U.S. Coast Guard.* Annapolis, MD: Naval Institute Press, 2010.

LaGuardia-Kotite, Martha J. *So Others May Live: Coast Guard's Rescue Swimmers: Saving Lives, Defying Death.* Guilford, CT: The Lyons Press, 2008.

Mitchell, Matthew. *Not Your Father's Coast Guard: The Untold Story of U.S. Coast Guard Special Forces.* Bloomington, IN: AuthorHouse, 2009.

Ostrom, Thomas P. *The United States Coast Guard: 1790 to the Present.* Oakland, OR: Elderberry Press, 2006.

Ostrom, Thomas P. *The United States Coast Guard in World War II: A History of Domestic and Overseas Actions.* Jefferson, NC: McFarland, 2009.

Randolph, Joanne. *Coast Guard Boats* (To the Rescue!) New York, NY: PowerKids Press, 2008.

Silverstein, Judy. *The U.S. Coast Guard and Military Careers*. Berkeley Heights, NJ: Enslow Publishers, 2007.

Stone, Lynn. *Coast Guard Cutters*. Vero Beach, FL: Rourke Publishing, 2006.

Thompson, Kalee. *Deadliest Sea: The Untold Story Behind the Greatest Rescue in Coast Guard History*. New York, NY: William Morrow, 2010.

Tougias, Michael J., and Casey Sherman. *The Finest Hours: The True Story of the U.S. Coast Guard's Most Daring Sea Rescue*. New York, NY: Scribner, 2009.

Walker, Spike. *On the Edge of Survival: A Shipwreck, a Storm, and the Harrowing Alaskan Rescue that Became a Legend*. New York, NY: St. Martin's Press, 2010.

Weintraub, Aileen. *First Response: By Sea*. Danbury, CT: Children's Press, 2007.

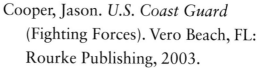

Cooper, Jason. *U.S. Coast Guard* (Fighting Forces). Vero Beach, FL: Rourke Publishing, 2003.

David, Jack. *United States Coast Guard*. London, England: Bellwether Media, 2008.

Demarest, Chris. *Mayday! Mayday! A Coast Guard Rescue*. New York, NY: Margaret McElderry, 2004.

Doane, Chris, and Joe DiRenzo III. "The Coast Guard's Value to the Nation." *The Coast Guard Outlook*, 2011. Retrieved February 10, 2011 (https://www.piersystem.com/external/content/document/786/977991/1/CG%20Outlook%202011%20Printed%20Publication.pdf).

The Grio. "La'Shanda Holmes, First Black Female Coast Guard Copter Pilot Flying High." The Grio, February 9, 2011. Retrieved February 10, 2011 (http://www.thegrio.com/black-history/thegrios-100/2011-lashanda-holmes.php).

Horne, Stacey. "Workers Taken Off Stricken North Sea Oil Platform." *Press and Journal*. Retrieved February 4, 2011 (http://www.pressandjournal. co.uk/Article.aspx/2123159#ixzz1DDOqQOW1).

Kirkham, Russell, AMTC Recruiter. Vancouver, Washington, January 29, 2011. In interview with the author.

Krietemeyer, George E. *The Coast Guardsman's Manual*. 9th ed. Annapolis, MD: Naval Institute Press, 2000.

Lyons, Lewis. *Rescue at Sea with the U.S. and Canadian Coast Guards*. Broomall, PA: Mason Crest Publishers, 2003.

Meininger, William. *Recollections of Thirty-Two Years in the U.S. Coast Guard and Other Ramblings*. Bloomington, IN: AuthorHouse, 2008.

Noble, Dennis L. *Lifeboat Sailors: The U.S. Coast Guard's Small Boat Stations*. Dulles, VA: Potomac Books, 2001.

Noble, Dennis L. *The U.S. Coast Guard*. New York, NY: Gareth Stevens Publishing, 2004.

Phillips, Donald T., and James M. Loy. *Character in Action: The U.S. Coast Guard on Leadership*. Annapolis, MD: United States Naval Institute, 2003.

Pinnero, Luke, Public Affairs Officer, 3rd Class. "Vertical Insertion Training." Coast Guard News Service, July 9, 2006. Retrieved February 9, 2011 (http://usmilitary.about.com/od/coastguard/a/vin-sertion.htm).

Sample, Doug, Sergeant 1st Class. "Coast Guard
Rescue Swimmer Training." American Forces Press
Service, September 12, 2004. Retrieved February 8,
2011 (http://usmilitary.about.com/od/coastguard/a/
cgrescueswimmer.htm).

Smith, Robert. "Coast Guard Uses Airboat
to Retrieve Ice Fishermen Disoriented
by Snowstorm." Cleveland Plain Dealer,
February 6, 2011. Retrieved February 7, 2011
(http://blog.cleveland.com/metro/2011/02/
coast_guard_uses_airboat_to_re.html).

U.S. Coast Guard. The Coast Guard Officer Career
Development Guidebook. 2nd ed. Retrieved
February 11, 2011 (http://www.uscg.mil/hq/cape-
may/education/doc/OCareerDevGuidebook.pdf).

U.S. Coast Guard. "Developing a Career as a Coast
Guard Officer." June 2007. Retrieved February
11, 2011 (http://www.uscg.mil/opm/opmdocs/
Developing_a_Career_as_a_CG_Officer.pdf).

Vogt, Tom. "Coast Guard Works to Stabilize Derelict."
Columbian, February 3, 2011. Retrieved February
4, 2011 (http://www.columbian.com/news/2011/
feb/03/coast-guard-works-to-stabilize-derelict).

INDEX

ABOUT THE AUTHOR

Tamra Orr is a writer and author living in the Pacific Northwest. She has written numerous nonfiction books for readers of all ages, including Rosen Publishing's *Your Career in the Navy*. Orr is the mother of four, and learning about the coast guard was fascinating for the entire family.

PHOTO CREDITS

Cover, back cover, pp. 1, 3, 8, 9, 14, 17, 21, 24, 33, 35, 40, 42, 43, 47, 49, 51, 53, 57, 59, 62, 66, 68, 70, 72, 75, 84, 86, 88–89, 92, 97, 101, 110 U.S. Coast Guard; pp. 5, 13, multiple interior graphics (climbing silhouettes) U. S. Navy; pp. 7, 22, 39, 48, 58, 67, 79, 94, multiple interior graphics (camouflage) Shutterstock.com; p. 107 © AP Images.

Designer: Les Kanturek; Photo Researcher: Amy Feinberg